ALEC CLIFTON-TAYLOR

TEWKESBURY

BRITISH BROADCASTING CORPORATION

The photographs in this book, apart from those listed below, were taken by Geoff Howard and reproduced from prints made by Michael Spry of Downtown Darkroom.

Acknowledgement is due to the following for permission to reproduce illustrations (the figures refer to plate numbers): Aerofilms, front cover; National Monuments Record, 17 (copyright Oxford City Library), 19.

The plan was drawn by ESR Ltd, cartographers.

Published by the
British Broadcasting Corporation
35 Marylebone High Street
London W1M 4AA

First published 1978 as a chapter in *Six English Towns*
This edition first published 1984
© Alec Clifton-Taylor 1978

ISBN 0 563 20297 1

Printed in England by
Jolly & Barber Ltd
Rugby, Warwickshire

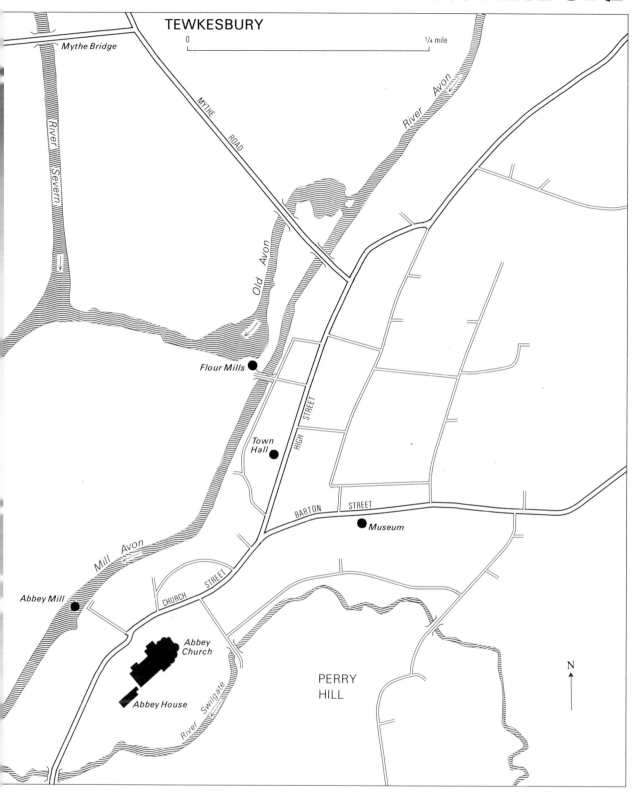

TEWKESBURY

TEWKESBURY

0   ¼ mile

Mythe Bridge

River Severn

River Avon

MYTHE ROAD

Old Avon

Flour Mills ●

HIGH STREET

Town Hall ●

BARTON STREET

Museum ●

Mill Avon

Abbey Mill ●

CHURCH STREET

Abbey Church

Abbey House

River Swilgate

PERRY HILL

N

1. Tewkesbury – town plan

Tewkesbury existed in Anglo-Saxon times, and in 800 one of the West Saxon Kings, Brictric, was buried here, in the first Abbey; but during the ninth century the Danes several times sailed up the Severn and plundered the monastery, which by 1000 had only five monks. Soon after this its status was reduced to that of a cell of Cranborne Abbey in Dorset. So Saxon Tewkesbury is unimportant, and nothing survives.

At the end of the eleventh century the feudal lord was Robert FitzHamon, a cousin of William Rufus. In 1102 he and Girald, the Abbot of Cranborne, decided – why is not known – to erect a new abbey church at Tewkesbury and to reduce Cranborne to priory status. The great new church was consecrated in 1121. So the town sprang up in the twelfth century, in the first place to serve the Benedictine monastery, whose church is still Tewkesbury's principal building. Among the English churches which are not cathedrals only Westminster Abbey and Beverley Minster are finer. It is predominantly a building of the twelfth and fourteenth centuries. From the earlier period the principal survivals are the tower (2), one of the largest and noblest built by the Normans (it once carried a wooden spire); the west front (4), the centre part of which steps forward no fewer than six times, in ever bolder and loftier arches; and, within, the huge circular piers of the nave (7), each $6\frac{1}{4}$ ft in diameter and nearly 31 ft high. In the twelfth century similar naves were built at Pershore and at Evesham, but today only the nave of Gloucester Cathedral is comparable.

. The Abbey from the south-east

For their continuing prosperity, all the medieval monasteries were largely dependent upon benefactors: and here Tewkesbury was lucky. A succession of noble patrons were lavish with their endowments: in the thirteenth century the De Clares, in the fourteenth the Despensers, and in the fifteenth the Beauchamps. All these in turn held the honour

4. *The West front*

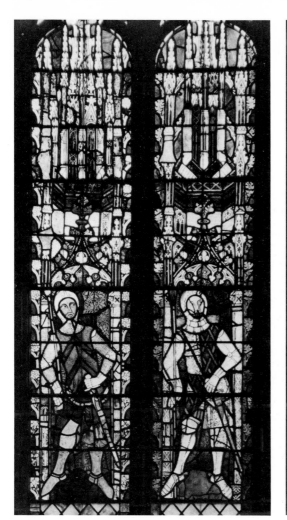

of Tewkesbury, an honour, in feudal times, being a group of manors held under one baron or lord: so they could well afford to give. But few monastic foundations received so much.

Eleanor, the last of the De Clares, married Hugh le Despenser, who, like the King, Edward II, with whom he had been much involved, was murdered. As a memorial to him, she gave the seven big windows of fourteenth-century stained glass in the clerestory of the sanctuary. Only the central window, the one facing east, has a subject: here is the Last Judgment, with the Resurrection below. Otherwise, each light has just a single figure: in the two eastern pairs, kings and prophets (6); in the western pair, knights connected with Tewkesbury, clad in armour and helms and wearing surcoats that are mainly yellow and red, against backgrounds of rich greens patterned with conventionalised flowers (5). Boldly designed figures like these are absolutely right for this lofty situation. Although the facial features are rendered with strength and conviction, they are not portraits. Only the arms on their surcoats identify them.

Like most Norman churches, Tewkesbury only had a wooden roof. The vault was given by Eleanor's son and daughter-in-law, Hugh le Despenser the younger and Elizabeth Montacute (who completed the work after his death in 1348). In the nave the vault, although fine in itself, is too low: it seems rammed down on to the great Norman piers like a lid. But east of the crossing the church was reconstructed in the fourteenth century, to its great architectural advantage (8). Here the vault, built of Cotswold limestone, is among the most perfect in England: a glorious enrichment. This is a lierne

7. *The nave looking west*

8. *The sanctuary*

vault – from the French word *lier*, to tie. The liernes are the short ribs which tie the main ones together, to produce an exquisitely ornamental design (31). At every point of junction is a carved boss, and all these bosses were originally painted and gilded. Then, after the battle of Tewkesbury in 1471 (the door of the sacristy is still covered with armour-plate – arm and leg-pieces – taken from soldiers lying dead on the battlefield), the Yorkists commemorated their victory over the Lancastrians by adding their emblem, a circle of gilded suns. What a lovely gesture!

Many of these grandees chose to be buried in the Abbey: some have not just tombs but chantry chapels. So fine indeed are the monuments here that Tewkesbury has been aptly described as 'the Westminster Abbey of the feudal baronage'. The best of all is that of the Despensers, Hugh and Elizabeth, which was clearly inspired by the even finer monument to Edward II at Gloucester. Here they lie, side by side, carved in alabaster (9): he, as so often, with a lion at his feet and she with a dog. The tabernacle which envelops them is believed to be of Beer limestone from Devon, brought here because it lends itself, as does no Cotswold stone, to the most intricate detail. It has not, alas, escaped the attentions of the vandals or of the religious fanatics: not one of a score or more of its statuettes has been permitted to survive. But even now it is one of the loveliest English monuments of the Middle Ages: delicate, complicated, subtle (10).

9. *Hugh and Elizabeth le Despenser*

At the Dissolution the town, to its eternal honour, paid Henry VIII £453 – a big sum in those days, equivalent to at least £60,000 today – to acquire the monastic parts. So the abbey church, now parish church, survives almost intact (3), a grand brooding presence

10. *Hugh le Despenser's monument*

11. *The Abbey Gatehouse*

constantly in view. Incidentally, it was with reference to this church that, in March 1877, William Morris wrote his famous letter protesting against mischievous over-restoration, which not only stopped it here but led to the foundation of that splendid body, the Society for the Protection of Ancient Buildings.

Everyone will be struck by the contrast between the church, which is built entirely of stone, and the town, in which stone is the exception. Nearly all the stone, oolitic lime-stone, came from quarries to the east of Tewkesbury: some from Bredon hill, which was the nearest (six to seven miles) and the rest from various quarries in the Cotswolds, not all of which have been identified. These might have been fifteen miles away: not an easy journey, although it was at least all downhill or on the level. In the twelfth century a little stone appears to have been brought from Caen, while for those parts of the tower formerly masked by steep roofs they brought sandstone, also by water, from the Forest of Dean.

Tewkesbury's other stone buildings are few, and nearly all close to the Abbey. There is the handsome early Tudor Gatehouse (11), faced with that unmistakably yellow lime-stone from Guiting in the Cotswolds. Next to it is the only other conventual building to have survived: Abbey House, formerly the Abbot's lodging or perhaps his guest house, and now the Vicarage. This, in its structure, is a fascinating mixture. Internally it can be seen to be still largely timber-framed, while the garden front, giving on to (and darkened by) a venerable cedar tree, is Georgian and of brick. But the north side, facing the churchyard, is of stone (12): there is a beautiful early Tudor oriel window in Cotswold oolite, but otherwise the walling is blue lias. It came from Twyning, two miles to the north, so this is Tewkesbury's only truly local stone; but it is so soft that it has decayed badly, and it would seem that hardly anybody else considered it to be worth using.

12. Abbey House

Across the churchyard is the former National School, begun in 1813, probably in Painswick stone, also from the Cotswolds. Almost the only other stone building is the Town Hall, built originally in 1788 but twice altered in the Victorian period. Both these

13 *(far left).*
The Abbey mill

14 *(left). The*
churchyard gates

are buildings of some distinction, but untypical of Tewkesbury, as, I feel, are the grandly ceremonial wrought-iron gates to the churchyard, presented in 1734 by Lord Gage, which were perhaps the work of William Edney, the leading smith of Bristol (14).

From the top of the Abbey tower, all of 205 steps up, the view is revealing. Until the Industrial Revolution a river was nearly always the key to an inland town's prosperity. When roads were bad, and in winter sometimes impassable, barges were the only convenient way of transporting bulky goods. For water transport Tewkesbury was very well sited, for only half a mile away across the meadows to the left there is another and much larger river, the Severn, into which, a short distance downstream, the Avon flows.

It may seem odd that the town was not built at the junction of the two rivers. The reason, which still applies, is because of flooding. Valley-beds were much more often water-logged in the Middle Ages than they are today; but even now the whole of these pastures is sometimes under water. That is why they are so lush. Such fertile land was excellent for corn growing, and corn was always important here. In fact, as early as the twelfth century the Avon was diverted to provide power for the Abbey mill.

The original water mill does not of course survive. What we see now is a late eighteenth-century replacement, with a weather-boarded addition not even as old as that (13). It is no longer used for its original purpose, nor are the malthouse and granary adjoining, which incorporate remains of the Abbey barn. But today there is another flour mill by the Avon that is far and away the biggest industrial building in the town.

Apart from corn, the principal industries before the seventeenth century were wool and the weaving of cloth. From the earliest days Tewkesbury also had a flourishing market. And William Camden, writing in 1586, tells us that this place was famous, too, for its smart, biting mustard. In fact, if you wanted to suggest that somebody was very strong, there was an old saying: 'He looks as if he lives on Tewkesbury mustard'.

15. View from the Abbey Tower

The town had rather an odd plan: long and narrow, with the three principal streets forming a Y (1). The reason was that it could not expand westwards across the Avon, nor even on the land immediately to the south of the Abbey, because of the danger of floods. And towards the east it was hemmed in by abbey lands and the manorial estate. So even in the Middle Ages this was always a congested place, densely built up (15). It was shortage of space which accounts for a special feature of Tewkesbury: the alleys. A good many still survive. Some are so narrow that upstairs the buildings on either side can be seen to be almost touching (16). And down the alleys, behind the main street houses, there might be a lofty hall: a workshop perhaps, or a barn.

Until the closing years of the seventeenth century Tewkesbury was a timber-framed town, and survivors are still plentiful. The most familiar is the House of the Nodding Gables, or of the Golden Key, in the High Street (17): one of those faintly intoxicated-looking buildings, with overhanging upper storeys – no fewer than four of them here – making their obeisance to passers-by. Here, it is true, the gables nod more than usual, the result of an accident. The ridge-pieces broke and had to be secured.

Apart from their undeniable picturesqueness, it used to be said that the chief reason why jetties were so popular was that they gave people more floor space upstairs – which is certainly true. In towns pinched for space like Tewkesbury, they would no doubt have been very welcome. Yet in fact the justification of the jetty was purely structural. Think of upstairs rooms full of furniture: heavy oak beds, tables, chests and so on. In due course the joists that carry these heavy pieces will be almost certain to sag. But if these joists project into space and are weighted at their outer ends by having to carry upper walls and part of the roof, the effect is one of counterpoise. Thus a jetty is actually a source not of weakness but of strength. Nor should it be forgotten that in the sixteenth century, when many of those houses went up, there were no gutters and no downpipes. The rain just poured off the roof. Lime-plaster is very vulnerable to rainwater. The jetties were also useful, therefore, in helping to throw the water clear of the walls. That in the process it spouted instead upon the heads of the passers-by was just too bad.

16 (far left). Ancil's Court

17 (left). The House of the Nodding Gables, an early photograph

16

In Tudor and Jacobean days the timbers would seem never to have been black. A permanent black was not to be had until tar and pitch, distilled from coal, became available, and that was associated with the industrial processes of the nineteenth century. When early oak timbers, later plastered over, are revealed again, the oak is always found to be in its natural state: that is to say, light brown or grey-brown. 'Black and white', which we associate mainly with the western counties and with the North, was essentially a Victorian fashion. It became so popular that sometimes, as can be seen at 22 Barton Street, the timbers, or at least some of them, are a sham, just painted on to brick.

My own decided preference is for the oak to be left in its natural state, unblacked. That is what we find at 64 Barton Street, a seventeenth-century house carefully restored to serve as a museum. The special feature of this house is the continuous range of sixteen casement windows with leaded lights on the first floor (18).

In the recent restoration of a long range of late-medieval houses now known as Abbey Cottages, in that part of Church Street backing on to the Abbey, it is a pity that thick, wooden glazing bars were introduced instead, for these do not look right, and here the oak timbers have been so drastically limewashed as to present a positively bleached appearance. With these two provisos the work can be warmly applauded. At a cost exceeding £100,000, a range which had become so dilapidated as to be in serious danger of demolition, on a site of vital importance to the town, has been saved for posterity (19). In the Georgian period two of the houses had been wholly, and two more partly, refronted: the former, quite rightly, have not been altered.

19. *Abbey Cottages*

Clarence House in the High Street, also late-medieval in origin, was reconstructed about 1630, when it lost two of its three original gables. But at that time was inserted, on the first floor, the finest plaster ceiling in Tewkesbury. With its wreaths, cherubs and central raspberry pendant, and its acanthus-leaf cornice with egg and dart mouldings, this ceiling is surprisingly sumptuous for so modest a house.

After the monastery was dissolved in 1539, the town, which so largely depended on it, lost a good deal of its prosperity, and it was not until the Georgian period that it really began to pick up again. The corn trade was still important, and so now were malting and leather goods, especially saddles; but there was no more cloth-weaving. Instead, the people took to knitting, which was done at home on frames. In 1723, Daniel Defoe, following the Severn from Gloucester, 'came to Tewksbury (sic), a large and very populous town, . . . famous for a great manufacture of stockings'. This was still true a century later, when one inhabitant in every four was knitting stockings.

Another flourishing industry now was brickmaking. Beside the Severn, where there was plenty of suitable clay, both above and below the town brickworks were started. So timber went right out. By the early years of the eighteenth century, everyone wanted brick.

Not everyone, however, could afford to rebuild. A good many houses in Tewkesbury which appear to be of Georgian brick are in fact only brick-fronted. The brickwork may, in fact, only be skin deep. A closer look will sometimes suggest clues. Take 79–80 Barton Street, formerly the Star and Garter, a coaching inn (20). The brick front carries a lead rainwater head dated 1715. But the windows are not three lights across and four up, as the standard, and best, Georgian practice prescribed. They are four lights by four, and that is because of the low rooms. For these are not Georgian rooms at all: they belong to the much earlier timber-framed structure. If we step through the arch and view the building from the back, the timbers are still very much in evidence.

Georgian builders had to contend with the effects of two very troublesome taxes, of which this house also provides a good illustration. The tax on windows, which was really no more than a clumsy and extremely inept form of property tax, was first levied in 1696, and was increased no fewer than six times between 1747 and 1808: it was not finally repeated until 1851. In addition, in 1746 a heavy excise duty was imposed upon glass. So, in order to escape these taxes, the less affluent were driven to blocking up window after window. That this building in Barton Street wears today rather a starved look is because no fewer than six windows were blocked, and still are. Nevertheless, the Georgian age was a prosperous time for Tewkesbury. In just over a century the population doubled: in 1723 it was 2866; in 1831, 5780.

There are some very pleasant brick houses in Church Street, including a short Crescent, but all the best are in the High Street. It is unfortunate that the ground floors of a good many of them have had to be converted into shops or offices. Most of the pleasures now are at first- and second-floor levels. One of the most enjoyable, upstairs, is the Swan Hotel (21). The gracious sash-framed windows not only preserve all their glazing bars but their original Crown glass too.

21. *The Swan Hotel*

Early window glass, like stained glass, had been blown in cylinders or muffs, which were split along their length and flattened out as they cooled. But for Crown glass the process was quite different. The glass-blower inserted his hollow pipe (the 'blowing-iron') into the furnace and drew out a globule of molten 'metal' (as he called it). Then, taking a wooden bat and keeping the iron spinning all the time, he gradually flattened out the red-hot globule until it became a large circular disc. It must have been wonderful to watch. Because it did not come into contact with any other surfaces while it was being made, Crown glass kept a natural fire-finish, which gave it a special brilliancy, a compensation for frequent optical distortion, caused by the disc being always somewhat thicker towards the centre. (The 'bull's eye' in the middle, from which at the last moment the end of the blowing-iron would be detached, was very properly discarded in the eighteenth century.) Crown glass, confined to lights of Georgian proportions, can often be identified by its glinting reflections. But for more than a century it has been unobtainable, having been completely supplanted by machine-produced glass in sheets large enough to need no glazing bars, which appeared just in time for the Crystal Palace of 1851.

We only have to walk along the High Street at Tewkesbury to realise what a wretched aesthetic deprivation the removal of Georgian glazing bars and the substitution of sheet glass have entailed. Kingsbury House (Nos. 39–40) (24), Avonside (No.63) (22) and

22. Avonside,
High Street

Riverside House (No. 66) (23) are all excellent examples of eighteenth-century brick-work. But at Kingsbury House all the windows except the two in the so-called Venetian style in the centre have been spoilt: the window openings are no more than dark, cavernous holes in the wall, featureless and devoid of character. At the other two houses the damage has fortunately been confined to the ground-floor windows, but even this is serious. At both these some compensation is provided by the unusual character of the fanlights over the doors.

A special feature of Tewkesbury's Georgian buildings is the key-block of moulded terracotta over the centre of each window. These blocks, which were usually painted white, display a variety of decorative motifs.

All these houses belong to the years of Tewkesbury's greatest prosperity, and provide a perfect foil to the less sophisticated character of much of the half-timbering.

Within, too, there are survivals of Georgian elegance. The Tudor House Hotel (No. 52), despite the handsome castellated-lead rainwater heads dated 1701, has a front disfigured with mock timber-framing in 1897 (26). It is therefore a delightful surprise, on entering, to find a very handsome Georgian staircase of impeccable proportions (25).

23. *Riverside House (now Hotel), High Street*

At last, about 1800, the condition of the roads began to improve, and brought an influx of new traffic. Tewkesbury had always been on the direct north-south route from the Midlands to Bristol, but up to this time the rivers were usually preferred for the transport of merchandise, and sometimes by travellers too. But, in addition to better

24 *(opposite). Kingsbury House, High Street*

roads, a great change was brought about in 1826 by the bridging of the Severn, where previously there had only been a ferry.

The designer of the Mythe Bridge was Thomas Telford, the greatest bridge-builder of the age. Before he was brought upon the scene in 1823, it was intended to have three arches. Telford found that the river bed was nothing but soft alluvial clay, so declared that the only solution was a single span. His design was carried out to the letter. The span is 170 feet, and on either side, he wrote, 'is a series of open arches, in place of solid masonry. I was led to this from having observed, in all the other cast-iron bridges constructed under my direction, that the great mass of solid masonry in the wings did not accord well with the openness of the ironwork; these arches are also of use when the floods rise more than three feet above the springing . . . As this is the first instance in which this mode has been adopted, I reckon this the handsomest bridge which has been built under my direction'[1] (27, 28).

[1] This quotation is taken from *A History of Tewkesbury* by James Bennett (1830: reprinted by Alan Sutton, 1976), pp. 288–9.

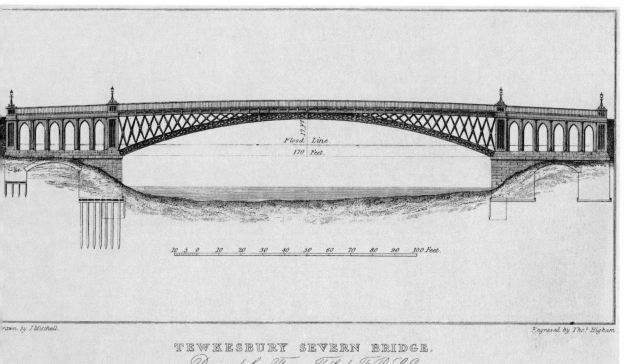

Drawn by J. Mitchell.   Engraved by Thos. Higham.

TEWKESBURY SEVERN BRIDGE.

Designed by Thomas Telford, F.R.S.E.

28. *The Mythe Bridge and Telford's design for it*

25

29. *The old Grammar Scho*

Since the year 1826 had already seen, on 30 January, the opening of a far more remarkable bridge by Telford, the Suspension Bridge over the Menai Straits, with a central span of 579 feet, which was easily the greatest in the world at that time, it is perhaps surprising that the opening of the Mythe Bridge should have been greeted with such excitement. Six years later the Grosvenor Bridge over the Dee at Chester, designed in 1827 by the veteran architect Thomas Harrison, was to achieve a span of 200 feet *in stone*, and to become, what it still remains, the boldest masonry arch in the kingdom. But at Tewkesbury Telford used cast iron, which, like the stone for the abutments, was floated down the river from Shropshire. The bridge brought the east-west traffic, going to Ledbury and Hereford. By 1830 thirty stage-coaches a day were either arriving at Tewkesbury or passing through. The House of the Nodding Gables became the ticket office for them. The inns flourished as never before.

But when, a few years later, the Birmingham to Bristol railway was built, it by-passed Tewkesbury and went through Ashchurch, where to this day many Tewkesbury people go to work. It is only two miles away, but that was far enough to result in the Industrial Revolution giving Tewkesbury a miss. The population in 1931 was actually 1400 less than a hundred years earlier. So there was practically no new building here between 1850 and 1930, which was visually, of course, a great piece of luck.

One building like the former Grammar School, now the Public Library (29), is surely quite enough – and all the more so as, by ill-fortune, it is situated nearly opposite the Abbey. It is built of machine-pressed bricks, probably from Ruabon – bricks made of hard, carbonaceous clay, faultless in their precision, relentless in their durability, pitiless in their colour. Needless to say these harsh reds were pointed with dark mortar. The machine-made tiles are equally rebarbative, while the typical cresting and the pair of cowls supply the final *coup de grâce*.

But there is an early Victorian façade in Tewkesbury which is very likeable: No. 124 High Street (30). The original house goes back to 1606 (hence the date above the

30. *124 High Street*

window), but in 1845 it was given a new front, in Gothick. The facing material is stucco, painted grey and white.

Since the last war, Tewkesbury has again become prosperous. (In 1981 the population was 9554.) This has brought with it one absolutely deplorable development in the High Street, carried out just before the whole of the old town was very properly designated a Conservation Area. But by and large the character of the place has been well preserved, and, perhaps partly owing to the diversion of much of the through traffic on to the M5 a mile and a half to the east, the buildings seem to be better maintained now than they used to be.

The appeal largely depends upon materials: the right materials in the right place. Oaks from nearby woods for timber-framing. Clay from the banks of the Severn for brick-making. Stone only for a few of the less private edifices: the Town Hall, the National School, the Gatehouse, and above all, of course, for the Abbey church, to which, here at Tewkesbury, our eyes and our thoughts continually return.

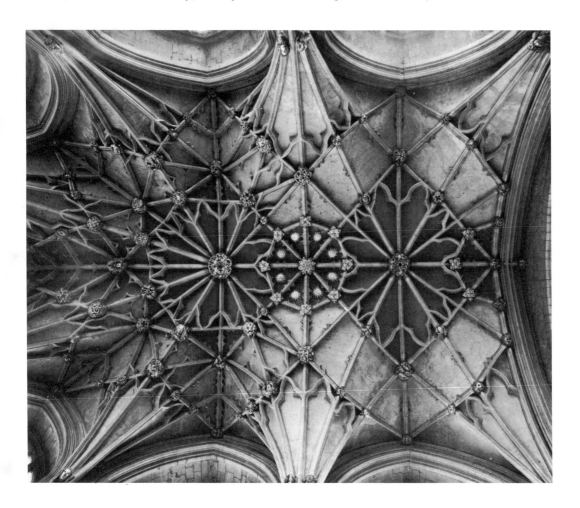

31. *Sanctuary vault, Tewkesbury Abbey*